I0817558

BEST OF MARCH MADNESS

MARCH MADNESS CINDERELLA STORIES

BY CHARLIE BEATTIE

abdobooks.com

Published by Abdo Publishing, a division of ABDO, PO Box 398166, Minneapolis, Minnesota 55439.

Printed in the United States of America, North Mankato, Minnesota.
102025
012026

Cover Photo: Elaine Thompson/AP Images, Focus On Sport/Getty Images, Wim McNamee/Getty Images Sport/Getty Images
Interior Photos: Zach Bolinger/Icon Sportswire/Getty Images, 4–5; Darron Cummings/AP Images, 6; Andy Lyons/Getty Images Sport/Getty Images, 9, 31, 38; Matt Rourke/AP Images, 11; NCAA Photos/Getty Images, 12–13; Rich Clarkson/NCAA Photos/Getty Images, 15; AP Images, 17; Tomy Tomsic/Sports Illustrated/Getty Images, 18; Mitchell Layton/Getty Images Sport/Getty Images, 20–21; Jed Jacobsohn/Getty Images Sport/Getty Images, 23; Eric Draper/AP Images, 25; Tom Hauck/Allsport/Getty Images Sport/Getty Images, 27; Jerry Holt/Star Tribune/Getty Images, 28–29; Robert Seale/Sporting News Archive/Getty Images, 33; Gregory Shamus/Getty Images Sport/Getty Images, 34; John Froschauer/AP Images, 36–37; Tony Gutierrez/AP Images, 40; Kevin C. Cox/Getty Images Sport/Getty Images, 43; Mike Fisher/AP Images, 44; Jessica Hill/AP Images, 45

Editor: Dalton Rains
Series Designer: Ebonee Estrella

Library of Congress Control Number: 2025939198

Publisher's Cataloging-in-Publication Data

Names: Beattie, Charlie, author.
Title: March Madness Cinderella stories / by Charlie Beattie
Description: Minneapolis, Minnesota: Abdo Publishing, 2026 | Series: Best of March Madness | Includes online resources and index.
Identifiers: ISBN 9781098298173 (lib. bdg.) | ISBN 9798384931973 (ebook)
Subjects: LCSH: Basketball--Juvenile literature. | College sports--Juvenile literature. | Basketball--Tournaments--United States--Juvenile literature. | College sports--United States--History--Juvenile literature. | NCAA Basketball Tournament--Juvenile literature. | March Madness (National Collegiate Athletic Association)--Juvenile literature.
Classification: DDC 796.32363--dc23

TABLE OF CONTENTS

25
KENTUCKY
10
SP
UK

CHAPTER ONE

SAINT PETER'S SURPRISE

Doug Edert curled around a screen and darted into the lane. The 6-foot, 2-inch guard had his eyes on the basket. His Saint Peter's Peacocks trailed the No. 2 seed Kentucky Wildcats 71–69 in the first round of the 2022 men's National Collegiate Athletic Association (NCAA) Tournament. Less than 30 seconds remained in the game.

Kentucky forward Oscar Tshiebwe blocked Edert's path. Forced to pull up, Edert lofted a floater over the 6-foot-9 defender's head. The shot dangled on the rim for a moment. Then it dropped through the basket. The game was tied. After a Kentucky miss at the other end of the court, the game went to overtime.

A Cinderella story happens when a low-seeded team makes an unexpected run. Heading into the

Saint Peter's guard Doug Edert (25) takes a shot against Kentucky in the 2022 men's NCAA Tournament.

Kentucky forward Oscar Tshiebwe, *right*, averaged 17.4 points and 15.1 rebounds per game in 2021–22.

2022 tournament, all signs had pointed toward an easy Kentucky win. Saint Peter's was a No. 15 seed. The tiny New Jersey school had been to the NCAA Tournament only three times and was winless in those appearances. Meanwhile, Kentucky was a basketball power with eight national championships. The team had been to the Final Four several times under coach John Calipari. A few of Kentucky's assistant coaches even made more money than Saint Peter's head coach, Shaheen Holloway. And the Wildcats' roster was stacked with top recruits.

Adding to Saint Peter's woes, the game was being played in Indianapolis, Indiana. Many Kentucky fans were able to make the trip to the neighboring state, filling the arena with Wildcat blue. Very few of Saint Peter's roughly 2,000 students made the trek from the school's Jersey City, New Jersey, campus. Many of them gathered in a large lecture hall to watch the game on a big screen instead.

Saint Peter's fought hard all game. Whenever Kentucky took a lead, the Peacocks answered with big baskets. The trend continued in overtime. Kentucky quickly took a four-point lead. But then a free throw from forward KC Ndefo and a three-pointer from Edert tied it back up. After that, Saint Peter's surged ahead. Guard Daryl Banks III led the team with 27 points. Edert finished with 20 more off the bench. And guard Matthew Lee sealed the upset with a pair of free throws in the last minute of overtime. As the final buzzer confirmed the 85–79 win, the students watching in New Jersey erupted.

MAKING HISTORY

The men's and women's NCAA Tournaments are nicknamed "March Madness." With 68 teams starting

THE 'STACHE

Due to the COVID-19 pandemic, Saint Peter's didn't play a game for 27 days during the 2021–22 season. The team didn't want to take risks, so the players mostly stayed to themselves. Matthew Lee cut his teammates' hair during that time. He also trimmed Doug Edert's facial hair into a thin mustache. Edert hit many big shots during the tournament. As Saint Peter's advanced, Edert's signature look became famous.

each tournament, the early rounds include a flurry of games. Whenever one of those games ends in an upset, fans across the nation take notice. Saint Peter's win over Kentucky was one of the biggest upsets in March Madness history. Since the men's tournament expanded to 64 teams in 1985, only nine No. 15 seeds had ever won a game. The Peacocks became the 10th entry on the list.

Despite the impressive first-round win, most fans expected the Saint Peter's run to end two days later. Only two No. 15 seeds had ever won a second-round game in the men's tournament. But the Peacocks weren't concerned with the past. They faced No. 7 seed Murray State next. The No. 15 seed jumped to a lead in the first half. The Racers tried to rally in the second half, but they couldn't catch up. The Peacocks never trailed as they pulled away for a 70–60 win.

Suddenly, the tiny New Jersey school was the talk of the tournament. Yet another massive test awaited in the Sweet 16. The Peacocks had a few days off before facing No. 3 seed Purdue. During that time, the national media hounded the Peacocks. Sportswriters and broadcasters turned Edert and Banks into stars. Saint Peter's went from an unknown school to a fan-favorite underdog.

The team wasn't satisfied with just two wins, though. The Peacocks showed up at the Sweet 16 wearing T-shirts that read, "More is Possible." This time, Saint Peter's had

Saint Peter's forward KC Ndefo (11) posted 17 points and 10 rebounds against Murray State.

many fans on hand. The game was played in Philadelphia, Pennsylvania, just 90 miles (145 km) from the school's campus. Purdue was led by 7-foot, 4-inch center Zach Edey and athletic guard Jaden Ivey. Saint Peter's attacked both stars all game. The Peacocks held Ivey to only nine points while forcing six turnovers from the guard.

But Purdue's defense was also holding strong. Saint Peter's trailed by two with just over three minutes to go. Then Banks hit a turnaround jump shot in the lane to tie it up. After the Peacocks got a defensive stop at the other end, Banks attacked the rim again. His floater dropped in the basket for a two-point lead.

The Peacocks held on to the advantage. With four seconds left, Edert drained two free throws to put his team up 67–64. Ivey received the inbounds pass for Purdue and quickly raced up the floor. He chucked up a long shot from beyond the top of the key. It hit the rim and bounced away. Saint Peter's had made history. No seed lower than No. 12 had ever made the Elite Eight.

After hitting clutch shots all tournament, Saint Peter's finally went cold against North Carolina. The team shot just 18-for-60 in a 69–49 loss. Despite the disappointing ending, it was an incredible two weeks for the small school. The NCAA Tournament had long been famous for its upsets and underdog stories. The Peacocks took the Cinderella dream further than any No. 15 seed ever had.

Guard Daryl Banks III (5) scored 14 points in Saint Peter's Sweet 16 victory over Purdue.

18

CHAPTER TWO

EARLY CINDERELLAS

The men's NCAA Tournament began in 1939. But for years, fewer than 30 teams took part in the competition each season. Only conference champions could appear in the tournament. Cinderella stories were rare.

By the 1980s, that had changed. The men's field grew to 40 teams in 1979. A few years later, the women's NCAA Tournament debuted with a field of 32 teams. More teams in the field meant more underdogs in matchups. And it didn't take long for one to step forward.

The Drake Bulldogs were only a No. 4 seed in the 1982 NCAA women's tournament. But the small school from Des Moines, Iowa, had a major offensive threat. The Bulldogs' leading scorer

Oregon beat Ohio State 46–33 in the 1939 men's NCAA championship game.

was 6-foot-3 Lorri Bauman. The star center mixed a stellar jump shot with fierce competitiveness. In the 1982 tournament, she put on a show for three games. Bauman overwhelmed No. 5 Ohio State in the first round with 34 points. The Bulldogs won 90–79.

Next up was No. 1 seed Long Beach State. Bauman led the way with 26 points and 11 rebounds to clinch a 91–78 upset. That put the Bulldogs just one win away from an unlikely spot in the first women's Final Four. Facing No. 2 seed Maryland, Bauman erupted. She hit 21 of her 35 shots from the field and finished with 50 points. More than 40 years later, that was still the record for a women's tournament game. Drake lost 89–78, but Bauman had delivered an incredible run.

SURVIVE AND ADVANCE

The 1983 men's NCAA Tournament was packed with loaded teams. Among all that talent, North Carolina State (NC State) didn't particularly stand out. The Wolfpack dealt with injuries in an up-and-down season. However, they managed to run the table to win the Atlantic Coast Conference (ACC) Tournament. NC State entered the 52-team NCAA Tournament as a No. 6 seed.

The Wolfpack kept the winning streak going. Along the way, Dereck Whittenburg and coach Jim Valvano established a ritual. After each win, the senior guard and excitable head coach found each other on the floor for a postgame hug.

The Wolfpack gutted out a 69–67 double-overtime win over Pepperdine in the first round. Then they took down No. 3 University of Nevada, Las Vegas (UNLV).

NC State guard Dereck Whittenburg (25) averaged 20.0 points per game in the 1983 NCAA Tournament.

Valvano and Whittenburg met for another hug after a 75–56 win over Utah in the Sweet 16. That set up an Elite Eight matchup with No. 1 seed Virginia. With seven minutes to go, the Wolfpack were down by seven points. Then NC State rallied to win 63–62. Whittenburg finished with 24 points.

After beating Georgia 67–60 in the Final Four, the Wolfpack went up against another No. 1 seed for the championship. This time it was Houston. NC State players knew they couldn't match the Cougars' athleticism. Valvano's best option was to slow the game down. At the time, there was no shot clock in college basketball. The Wolfpack held the ball as long as possible. Their long possessions made it a low-scoring matchup.

With the game tied 52–52 in the final seconds, NC State passed the ball around for nearly a minute. Then Whittenburg had to scramble for a loose ball near midcourt. He turned and heaved a long shot. It came up short. But forward Lorenzo Charles was there to catch the air ball. In one motion, Charles grabbed the ball and dunked it.

Valvano sprinted onto the court, looking for Whittenburg. But the senior guard was already hugging his teammates. Valvano went zigzagging around the court, looking for his star player. The scene became one of the NCAA Tournament's most famous images.

Jim Valvano and NC State celebrate after winning the 1983 men's national championship.

THE EXPANSION CREW

In the fall of 1981, three freshmen arrived at Villanova with big dreams. Center Ed Pinckney and guards Dwayne McClain and Gary McLain called themselves "The Expansion Crew." They planned to bring home a championship for the Wildcats.

However, the trio fell short in their first three seasons. They had reached the Elite Eight twice but had gone no further. Finally, in 1985, the three seniors struggled through a tough 19–10 season in the Big East.

In earlier years, the Wildcats might have missed the NCAA Tournament. But the field expanded to 64 teams in 1985. Villanova made it in as a No. 8 seed. The Expansion Crew had one last shot, but it was a long one.

The Wildcats didn't waste their opportunity. Villanova played stifling defense. Throughout a thrilling five-game

Villanova guard Dwayne McClain averaged 15 points per game in the 1985 men's NCAA Tournament.

run to the championship game, the Wildcats held every opponent to 55 points or fewer.

Villanova became the talk of the tournament. But conference rival Georgetown waited in the championship game. The Hoyas, led by star center Patrick Ewing, were the defending champions and had already beaten Villanova in two close games during the regular season. Those previewing the game didn't debate who would win; they just wondered how badly Villanova would lose.

The Wildcats came out playing loose and free. And they seemingly couldn't miss. Villanova shot a tournament-record 79 percent from the field. Pinckney outscored Ewing 16–14. Meanwhile, Dwayne McClain led all scorers with 17 points. And teammate Gary McLain's masterful dribbling dismantled Georgetown's famous swarming defense. When the final buzzer sounded, Villanova had done what many thought was impossible. The Wildcats won 66–64. Four decades later, they remained the lowest seed to ever win either the men's or the women's tournament.

DANNY AND THE MIRACLES

Kansas entered the 1988 men's NCAA Tournament as an unassuming No. 6 seed. But the Jayhawks also had one of the biggest stars in college basketball. Senior forward Danny Manning scored at least 20 points in each of the team's six tournament games. He piled up three double-doubles, including a 31-point, 18-rebound performance against No. 1 Oklahoma in the championship game. Kansas won 83–79 to capture the school's first title since 1952. Along the way, the team earned the nickname "Danny and the Miracles."

CHAPTER THREE

ON THE RISE

Cheryl Burnett began coaching the Southwest Missouri State (now known as Missouri State) women's basketball team in 1987. She took over a struggling program. The hardships continued after she arrived. In Burnett's first two years, the team had a combined record of 16–37. But the coach kept working. In 1991, the Bears reached the NCAA Tournament for the first time. They lost in the second round to eventual champion Tennessee. But legendary coach Pat Summitt called Southwest Missouri State the best defensive team Tennessee had played all season.

The Bears carried the confidence from that comment into the next year. They finished the 1991–92 regular season with a 25–2 record. But for a team playing in the small Gateway Conference, that was only good enough for a No. 8 seed. After an

Cheryl Burnett coached at Southwest Missouri State from 1987 to 2002.

opening-round win against No. 9 seed Kansas, the Bears had to face No. 1 seed Iowa.

Southwest Missouri State defenders smothered shots and forced turnovers. Behind that active defense, the Bears forced overtime. Then forward Secelia Winkfield banked in a short jumper with 1.5 seconds left to deliver a thrilling 61–60 win. At the time, it was one of the biggest upsets in women's tournament history.

The Bears headed into the Sweet 16 filled with confidence. They routed No. 5 University of California, Los Angeles (UCLA), 83–57. Then they took down No. 2 seed Ole Miss 94–71 to reach the Final Four. Southwest Missouri State's run ended there with an 84–72 loss against Western Kentucky. But the run marked the beginning of a new era. Burnett turned the Bears from a Cinderella into a strong national contender. By the time the coach left the program in 2002, she had led the team to eight more NCAA Tournaments.

GOOD MORNING AMERICA

The women's NCAA Tournament was well-established by 1998. However, unlike in the men's tournament, Cinderella runs were rare. Other than Southwest Missouri State's dash to the Final Four in 1992, low seeds rarely made much noise. That wasn't a good sign for the 1998 Arkansas Razorbacks. Coach Gary Blair's team finished just 17–9 in the regular season. The Razorbacks were a No. 9 seed. They also had to travel across the country to begin the tournament in Palo Alto, California.

In the first round, Arkansas gutted out a 76–70 win over Hawaii. The Razorbacks caught a break when No. 16 seed Harvard stunned No. 1 Stanford in a historic upset. Facing the Crimson in the second round, the Razorbacks cruised to an 82–64 win.

Arkansas then made the short trip to Oakland, California, for the Sweet 16. The Razorbacks outscored No. 5 seed Kansas 51–31 in the second half.

Arkansas center Tennille Adams averaged 6.8 points per game in 1997–98.

The Cinderella team won 79–63. Since California's time zone is two hours behind Arkansas, many fans didn't stay up late enough to catch the games. Instead, they got the results from the morning news. As the Razorbacks kept advancing, they became known as "Good Morning America's Team."

Arkansas faced its toughest test in the Elite Eight. No. 2 seed Duke was a heavy favorite, but the Razorbacks hung in all game. Reserve center Tennille Adams hit a go-ahead basket with just over a minute and a half remaining in the second half. Guard Christy Smith took over from there. The senior hit four free throws in the final seconds to seal a 77–72 upset. Arkansas's run ended in the Final Four against Southeastern Conference (SEC)

THE HARD WAY

The Arizona Wildcats were a No. 4 seed in the 1997 men's NCAA Tournament. Though they weren't serious underdogs, the Wildcats faced a tough road to the national title. Arizona beat No. 1 Kansas in the Sweet 16. Then the Wildcats knocked off two more No. 1 seeds in the Final Four. They beat North Carolina in the semifinals and Kentucky in the final. Arizona became the first team to beat three No. 1 seeds in the same tournament.

Arizona beat Kentucky 84–79 in the 1997 men's national championship game.

rival Tennessee. But Good Morning America's Team had captured the nation's attention.

THE SLIPPER FITS

Gonzaga entered the 1999 men's NCAA Tournament as a No. 10 seed. In the opening round, the Bulldogs completed a minor upset by beating No. 7 Minnesota 75–63. Even that was a historic step for the small school based in Spokane, Washington. Until then, Gonzaga had never won an NCAA Tournament game. In Gonzaga's only previous appearance four years earlier, the team had been blown away 87–63 by No. 3 seed Maryland. Around that time, Gonzaga was considering dropping out of Division I to face easier competition.

The Bulldogs' first-round win didn't raise many eyebrows. But Gonzaga's second-round upset of No. 2 Stanford put the entire country on notice. Led by the backcourt of Quentin Hall, Matt Santangelo, and Richie Frahm, Gonzaga shot 11-of-20 from three-point range. The Bulldogs won 82–74. With five days between that game and Gonzaga's Sweet 16 matchup against No. 3 Florida, the national media latched on to the Cinderella team.

Gonzaga's first two games had been played just a few hours away in Seattle. Then the team had to travel to Phoenix, Arizona, for the Sweet 16. The Bulldogs' hot shooting traveled there too. Frahm drained five three-point shots against the Gators. The rest of the team added seven more from long range.

Despite the hot shooting, Gonzaga trailed 72–71 in the final minute. Hall drove into the lane and missed a running bank shot. However, forward Casey Calvary crashed the board and tipped the ball in the basket. The Bulldogs snagged a one-point lead with 4.4 seconds to go. Florida missed a desperation shot at the buzzer, and television announcer Gus Johnson shouted, "The slipper still fits!"

The play, along with Johnson's call, instantly became part of NCAA Tournament lore.

Gonzaga was finally beaten by the eventual champion University of Connecticut (UConn) Huskies in a hard-fought Elite Eight battle. But the 1999 run was just the beginning of the Bulldogs' story. In the coming years, they went from underdogs to national powers. In 2025, Gonzaga appeared in its 26th straight NCAA Tournament.

Gonzaga forward Casey Calvary dunks the ball during the 1999 Sweet 16.

MINNESOTA
13

CHAPTER FOUR

NEW CENTURY, NEW STORIES

Early in the 2003–04 season, Minnesota's women's team looked like a real contender. Coach Pam Borton's squad started the season 15–0. But after an injury to star point guard Lindsay Whalen, the Golden Gophers lost eight of their final 14 games. When the NCAA Tournament rolled around, they were assigned a No. 7 seed.

Whalen got back to full strength at the perfect time. In the first round, the Minnesota native put up 31 points and nine assists. The Gophers topped UCLA 92–81. In the next round against No. 2 seed Kansas State, Minnesota center Janel McCarville piled up 15 points, 18 rebounds, and seven assists. The Gophers routed the Wildcats 80–61. A few days later, Whalen and McCarville posted double-doubles in the

Minnesota guard Lindsay Whalen posted a 47.4 field goal percentage in the first round of the 2004 NCAA Tournament.

Sweet 16. Minnesota pulled off another upset by taking down No. 3 Boston College 76–63.

The win put Minnesota into the Elite Eight for the first time in school history. The Gophers faced No. 1 seed Duke. Minnesota's star duo carried the team again. McCarville had 20 points, 18 rebounds, and six assists. Meanwhile, Whalen led all scorers with 27 points. She made a layup with under a minute to play that put the Gophers up by four, then added two clutch free throws to help clinch an 82–75 win. Minnesota's run ended in the Final Four when UConn bottled up the two stars. Nonetheless, the Gophers had treated fans to a spectacular two-woman Cinderella show.

BY GEORGE!

Few fans paid attention when George Mason entered the 2006 men's NCAA Tournament as a No. 11 seed. Only one No. 11 seed had ever made it to the Final Four. But that was the 1986 LSU Tigers, a major school from the SEC. George Mason of Fairfax, Virginia, was the regular season champion of the Colonial Athletic Association (CAA) in 2006. No team from the small conference had ever come close to the Final Four. George Mason also started the NCAA Tournament without one of its best players. Coach Jim Larrañaga had suspended point guard Tony Skinn for one game for punching an opponent

George Mason guard Folarin Campbell posted 21 points and seven rebounds in the first round of the 2006 men's NCAA Tournament.

during the CAA tournament. Against those odds, George Mason took down No. 6 Michigan State in the first round. Skinn returned for round two. The Patriots then upset defending champion North Carolina 65–60.

George Mason's Sweet 16 and Elite Eight games were scheduled for the Verizon Center in Washington, DC. The arena was just 20 miles (32 km) from the school's campus. Fans turned out in huge numbers as George Mason took down No. 7 Wichita State in the Sweet 16.

Next up was No. 1 seed UConn. The Huskies were loaded with talent. Their roster included four future first-round National Basketball Association (NBA) Draft picks, and coach Jim Calhoun's team had won the tournament just two years before. George Mason, which didn't often go deep into its bench, didn't seem to have much of a chance. Nonetheless, the Patriots stuck with the Huskies all game. George Mason's starting five played the final 10:37 of the second half. The Patriots led by two in the closing seconds, but UConn tied the game on a layup as the buzzer sounded, forcing overtime. George Mason's starters then played all five minutes of overtime. The underdogs took an 85–80 lead in the extra period. But they struggled to hit free throws to close out the game.

THE WRONG GEORGE

More than 3 million fan brackets were submitted to popular sports website ESPN before the 2006 men's NCAA Tournament. Only four of them predicted that George Mason would reach the Final Four. One of the lucky four was made by Russell Pleasant from Omaha, Nebraska. When interviewed about his bold prediction, Pleasant admitted he thought he was picking George Washington. The similarly named school is in Washington, DC, not far from George Mason.

Guard Tony Skinn scored 14 points in George Mason's 2006 Sweet 16 matchup against Wichita State.

After cutting the lead to two, UConn had another chance. Huskies forward Denham Brown launched a three-pointer at the buzzer. It missed. The Patriots escaped with an 86–84 win, earning a trip to the Final Four. George Mason's season ended in the next game at the hands of eventual champion Florida, but the Patriots had completed one of the most remarkable Cinderella runs in NCAA history.

Davidson guard Steph Curry averaged 32.0 points per game in the 2008 NCAA Tournament.

SHOOTER'S TOUCH

In 2008, Steph Curry was a short, skinny point guard playing for the Davidson Wildcats. The sophomore had averaged more than 25 points per game that season. But few noticed the star as his team ran through the lesser-known Southern Conference. He finally gained national attention by torching No. 7 seed Gonzaga with 40 points in the first round of the NCAA Tournament.

Curry scored 30 in the second half alone. The guard's eight three-pointers locked down an 82–76 win for the No. 10 seed Wildcats.

In the second round, Davidson played Georgetown. Curry made five more three-pointers against the No. 2 seed. He scored 30 points to help Davidson erase a 46–29 second-half deficit to win 74–70.

Davidson offered its 1,700 students free bus tickets from North Carolina to Detroit, Michigan, to see Curry and the Wildcats take on Wisconsin in the Sweet 16. Davidson head coach Bob McKillop estimated that about 1,200 took the offer. Also in attendance was superstar LeBron James, then in his fifth NBA season.

The audience witnessed another Curry spectacular. The teams were tied 36–36 at halftime. Then Curry overcame Wisconsin's top-ranked defense to finish with 33 points, including six long-range makes. Davidson pulled away to win 73–56.

Eventual champion Kansas smothered Curry with double teams in the Elite Eight. Despite the pressure, the sophomore still scored 25 points and the Wildcats came within a shot of the Final Four. Despite his team's 59–57 loss, the Cinderella run was only the beginning of Steph Curry's legend, as he went on to become an NBA star. Some consider Curry to be the best pure shooter in basketball history.

GONZAGA
21

CHAPTER FIVE

MODERN RUNS

In 2011, Texas A&M emerged as one of the NCAA Tournament's most unlikely champions. However, before the Aggies won, the story of the tournament had been Gonzaga. Led by future Women's National Basketball Association (WNBA) superstar Courtney Vandersloot's 34 points, the No. 11 seed Bulldogs rallied from seven points down at halftime to beat No. 6 Iowa 92–86 in the first round. In the next round, Vandersloot scored 29 points in an 89–75 win over No. 3 seed UCLA. Gonzaga then beat No. 2 seed Louisville 76–69 in the Sweet 16. In the Elite Eight, Stanford finally shut down Gonzaga 83–60.

While Gonzaga was making its run through the women's field, several low seeds were making waves in the men's tournament. Five teams seeded No. 8 or lower reached the Sweet 16. By the Final Four, not a single No. 1 or No. 2 seed was left standing.

Gonzaga guard Courtney Vandersloot averaged 29.3 points per game in the 2011 women's NCAA Tournament.

One of the teams that went on a crazy ride was Virginia Commonwealth University (VCU). In 2011, the NCAA Tournament expanded to 68 teams. Eight teams played in the First Four, a collection of four games to get the field down to 64. VCU, a No. 11 seed, was one of them. The Rams knocked out the University of

In the 2011 men's NCAA Tournament, Butler guard Shelvin Mack averaged 20.3 points per game.

Southern California (USC). Then they upset No. 6 seed Georgetown 74–56 and No. 3 Purdue 94–76. A slim 72–71 victory over No. 10 Florida State in the Sweet 16 lifted the Rams to the Elite Eight.

VCU continued its upset run by beating No. 1 Kansas 71–61 to reach the Final Four. Waiting in the semifinals was yet another Cinderella team. Butler University, a small school in Indiana, had finished as national runners-up in 2010 as a No. 5 seed. Now they were a No. 8 seed. The Bulldogs had already upset No. 1 Pittsburgh, No. 4 Wisconsin, and No. 2 Florida.

Butler won the all-Cinderella semifinal 70–62. After that, the Bulldogs faced No. 3 seed UConn in the title game. The Huskies closed out one of the wildest NCAA Tournaments ever with a 53–41 win.

DUNK CITY

Just seven years before the 2013 men's NCAA Tournament, Florida Gulf Coast University (FGCU) had competed in Division II. In 2012–13, the Eagles had posted a 15–17 record. Coach Andy Enfield's team only clinched a spot in the 2013 NCAA Tournament after upsetting Mercer in the Atlantic Sun Conference Tournament final.

The Eagles were handed a No. 15 seed and faced No. 2 Georgetown in the first round. FGCU led by five early in the second half. Then the Eagles sprinted out

Florida Gulf Coast forward Eddie Murray dunks the ball during the 2013 men's NCAA Tournament.

on a fast break. Point guard Brett Comer threw up a lob for forward Chase Fieler. The 6-foot-8 junior finished off the alley-oop and drew a huge roar from the crowd in Philadelphia.

Three minutes later, Comer drove the lane for a layup attempt. He missed, but senior forward Eddie Murray followed up with another rim-rattling dunk. Murray and Fieler both added dunks as FGCU pulled away with a 21–2 run.

In the game's final minutes, Comer and Fieler added even more highlights. With the Eagles up by seven, Comer drove to the baseline. He flipped a no-look, underhand pass high above the basket. Fieler leaped, grabbed the ball with one hand, and hammered it through the hoop. FGCU won 78–68, and the legend of "Dunk City" was born.

The Eagles became the seventh No. 15 seed to win a first-round game. They hoped to become the first to win in the second round. Facing No. 7 San Diego State, FGCU threw down another six dunks. Four of them came from 6-foot-9 forward Eric McKnight. With each slam, the "Dunk City" legend grew. Guard Bernard Thompson scored a game-high 23 points as FGCU won 81–71.

By the time the Eagles reached the Sweet 16 a few days later, their dunks had made the underdog team the talk of the sports world. No. 3 seed Florida was waiting. FGCU slammed down a pair of alley-oops to take an early 21–11 lead. But the Gators slowed down the Eagles the rest of the way, ending the run in a 62–50 win.

HUSKIES HEROES

The Washington Huskies were a No. 7 seed in the 2016 women's NCAA Tournament. But guard Kelsey Plum had at least 23 points in four straight tournament wins. The Huskies upset No. 2 Maryland, No. 3 Kentucky, and No. 4 Stanford. Syracuse finally took them down in the semifinals.

CHICAGO CLUTCH

In 2018, Loyola University Chicago appeared in the men's NCAA Tournament for the first time in 33 years. The team was assigned a lowly No. 11 seed. The Ramblers were an unselfish offensive team. They were also one of the top defensive units in the country. Plus, they seemed to have a good-luck charm. As the team took on the No. 6 seed Miami Hurricanes in the first round, television cameras often focused on a 98-year-old woman sitting next to the Ramblers' bench. By the second half, fans across the country were familiar with Sister Jean Schmidt, Loyola's team chaplain. Loyola trailed Miami 62–61 with nine seconds left. After a missed free throw by the Hurricanes, the Ramblers raced down the floor. Marques Townes fed fellow guard Donte Ingram near the top of the key. Ingram hit a buzzer-beating three-pointer.

The Ramblers faced No. 3 Tennessee in the second round. Once again, Loyola trailed 62–61 in the final seconds. Star guard Clayton Custer dribbled around a screen and heaved up a desperation shot. The ball bounced off the front of the rim, then hit the backboard and dropped in with 3.6 seconds remaining. The shot held up as the winner when the Volunteers missed a three-pointer at the buzzer.

Loyola moved on to face Nevada in the Sweet 16 in Atlanta. Sister Jean traveled there too. She watched from the sideline as the Ramblers endured yet another close game. This time, Loyola led 66–65 with under 10 seconds left. Custer drove toward the basket and kicked a pass out to Townes. The junior drilled a three-pointer and Loyola held on for a 69–68 win.

The Ramblers didn't need any last-second heroics in the Elite Eight. They beat No. 9 Kansas State 78–62 to reach the Final Four for the first time in 55 years. As with most Cinderella bids, Loyola's eventually ended. The Ramblers lost 69–57 to Michigan in the Final Four. But Loyola's four-game run packed in enough memorable moments to satisfy fans for years.

Guard Ben Richardson, *center*, scored a game-high 23 points in Loyola's 2018 Elite Eight victory over Kansas State.

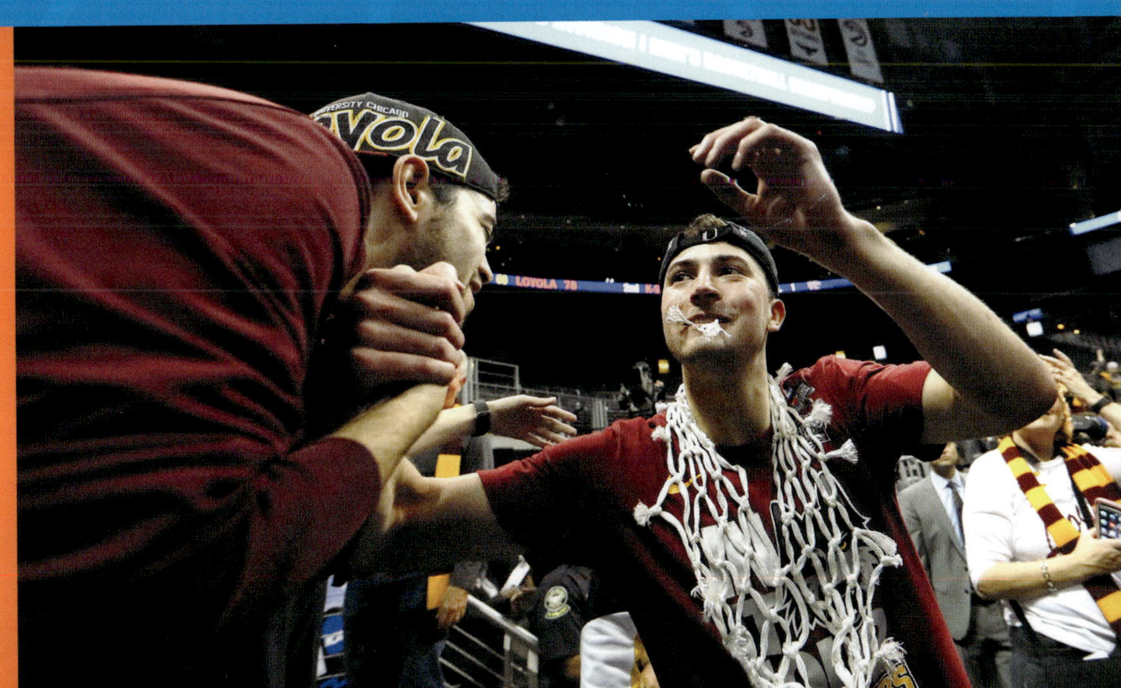

HONORABLE MENTIONS

1986 LSU MEN

The LSU Tigers snuck into the 1986 tournament as a No. 11 seed. Once there, they had last-second victories over No. 3 seed Memphis and No. 1 Kentucky on the way to becoming the first double-digit seed to reach the Final Four.

1989 MICHIGAN MEN

Michigan was a No. 3 seed in 1989, but the Wolverines were thrown a major curveball just before the tournament. Coach Bill Frieder was fired two days before Michigan's first tournament game. With assistant Steve Fisher in charge, Michigan ran the table and won its first ever national title. The Wolverines beat Seton Hall 80–79 in overtime in the final.

Steve Fisher

1994 TEXAS A&M WOMEN

In 1994, Texas A&M was a No. 13 seed. However, the team got to play No. 4 Florida at home in the first round because of a concert in the Gators' arena. The Aggies rode their home-court advantage to a 78–76 win. Texas A&M then beat San Diego State 75–72 in overtime to reach the Sweet 16.

Sabrina Ionescu

2017 OREGON WOMEN

In 2017, two star freshmen led Oregon to its first NCAA Tournament in 12 years. Center Ruthy Hebard blocked a last-second shot to help lift the No. 10 seed Ducks over Temple 71–70 in the first round. Next, she led Oregon to a 74–65 win over No. 2 Duke. Guard Sabrina Ionescu then scored 21 points as the Ducks upset No. 3 seed Maryland 77–63 in the Sweet 16. Oregon became the second women's No. 10 seed to reach the Elite Eight.

2023 MIAMI WOMEN

In the first round of the 2023 NCAA Tournament, No. 9 seed Miami pulled off a 17-point comeback to beat No. 8 seed Oklahoma State 62–61. In the next game, the Hurricanes beat No. 1 seed Indiana 70–68. They then held off Villanova 70–65 and became the second women's No. 9 seed to ever reach the Elite Eight.

2024 NC STATE MEN

In 2024, the NC State Wolfpack lost 10 of their final 14 regular-season games. But the team made a stunning run to the ACC Tournament title by winning five games in five days. That got them into the NCAA Tournament as a No. 11 seed. Led by 6-foot-9 forward D. J. Burns, the Wolfpack rolled to the Elite Eight. Then they upset ACC rival Duke 76–64 to grab a spot in the Final Four.

GLOSSARY

assist
A pass that leads directly to a basket.

chaplain
A person who performs religious work for a hospital, school, prison, or military.

contender
A person or team that has a good chance at winning a championship.

debut
First appearance.

double-double
Accumulating 10 or more of two certain statistics in a game.

draft
A system that allows teams to acquire new players coming into a league.

key
The area including the free-throw lane and free-throw circle.

overtime
An extra period of play when the score is tied after regulation.

pandemic
A widespread outbreak of a disease that affects a large portion of the population.

recruit
A player who is convinced to go to a specific school.

rival
An opponent with whom a player or team has a fierce and ongoing competition.

screen
A legal block by an offensive player against a defender to open up a teammate for a shot or a pass.

seed
A rank assigned to a player or team in a tournament.

underdog
The person or team that is not expected to win.

MORE INFORMATION

BOOKS

Big Book of Who Women in Sports: The 101 Stars Every Fan Needs to Know. Triumph, 2025.

Hanlon, Luke. *Everything Basketball.* Abdo, 2025.

Mahoney, Brian. *GOATs of Basketball.* Abdo, 2022.

ONLINE RESOURCES

To learn more about March Madness Cinderella stories, please visit **abdobooklinks.com** or scan this QR code. These links are routinely monitored and updated to provide the most current information available.

INDEX

ABOUT THE AUTHOR

Charlie Beattie is a writer, editor, and former sportscaster. Originally from Saint Paul, Minnesota, he now lives in Charleston, South Carolina, with his wife and son.